EVERMORE
from BEAUTY AND THE BEAST

CELLOS

Music by ALAN MENKEN
Lyrics by TIM RICE

FRIEND LIKE ME

from ALADDIN

CELLOS

Music by ALAN MENKEN
Lyrics by HOWARD ASHMAN

HEIGH-HO

The Dwarfs' Marching Song from SNOW WHITE AND THE SEVEN DWARFS

CELLOS

Words by LARRY MOREY
Music by FRANK CHURCHILL

Moderately, in 2

HOW FAR I'LL GO

from MOANA

CELLOS

Music and Lyrics by
LIN-MANUEL MIRANDA

Moderately, in 2

LET IT GO
from FROZEN

CELLOS

Music and Lyrics by KRISTEN ANDERSON-LOPEZ
and ROBERT LOPEZ

MICKEY MOUSE MARCH

from THE MICKEY MOUSE CLUB

CELLOS

Words and Music by
JIMMIE DODD

March tempo

Disney SONGS FOR TWO

Arrangements by Mark Phillips

ISBN 978-1-5400-3714-5

Visit Hal Leonard Online at
www.halleonard.com

Contact Us:
Hal Leonard
7777 West Bluemound Road
Milwaukee, WI 53213
Email: info@halleonard.com

In Europe contact:
Hal Leonard Europe Limited
42 Wigmore Street
Marylebone, London, W1U 2RN
Email: info@halleonardeurope.com

In Australia contact:
Hal Leonard Australia Pty. Ltd.
4 Lentara Court
Cheltenham, Victoria, 3192 Australia
Email: info@halleonard.com.au

BEAUTY AND THE BEAST
from BEAUTY AND THE BEAST

CELLOS

Music by ALAN MENKEN
Lyrics by HOWARD ASHMAN

Moderately slow

BIBBIDI-BOBBIDI-BOO
(The Magic Song)
from CINDERELLA

CELLOS

Words by JERRY LIVINGSTON
Music by MACK DAVID
and AL HOFFMAN

Brightly, in 2

6

CAN YOU FEEL THE LOVE TONIGHT
from THE LION KING

CELLOS

Music by ELTON JOHN
Lyrics by TIM RICE

Slowly, in 2

CHIM CHIM CHER-EE

from MARY POPPINS

CELLOS

Words and Music by RICHARD M. SHERMAN
and ROBERT B. SHERMAN

CIRCLE OF LIFE

from THE LION KING

CELLOS

Music by ELTON JOHN
Lyrics by TIM RICE

COLORS OF THE WIND

from POCAHONTAS

CELLOS

Music by ALAN MENKEN
Lyrics by STEPHEN SCHWARTZ

Moderately

WHO'S AFRAID OF THE BIG BAD WOLF?

from THREE LITTLE PIGS

CELLOS

Words and Music by
FRANK CHURCHILL
Additional Lyric by ANN RONELL

Moderately, in 2

A WHOLE NEW WORLD

from ALADDIN

CELLOS

Music by ALAN MENKEN
Lyrics by TIM RICE

Moderately

YOU'LL BE IN MY HEART
(Pop Version)
from TARZAN®

CELLOS

Words and Music by
PHIL COLLINS

Moderately

YOU'RE WELCOME

from MOANA

CELLOS

Music and Lyrics by
LIN-MANUEL MIRANDA

ZIP-A-DEE-DOO-DAH

from SONG OF THE SOUTH

Words by RAY GILBERT
Music by ALLIE WRUBEL

CELLOS

SOME DAY MY PRINCE WILL COME

from SNOW WHITE AND THE SEVEN DWARFS

CELLOS

Words by LARRY MOREY
Music by FRANK CHURCHILL

SOMETHING THERE
from BEAUTY AND THE BEAST

CELLOS

Music by ALAN MENKEN
Lyrics by HOWARD ASHMAN

SUPERCALIFRAGILISTICEXPIALIDOCIOUS

from MARY POPPINS

CELLOS

Words and Music by RICHARD M. SHERMAN
and ROBERT B. SHERMAN

Fast, in 2

D.C. al Fine

WHEN SHE LOVED ME

from TOY STORY 2

CELLOS

Music and Lyrics by
RANDY NEWMAN

WHEN YOU WISH UPON A STAR

from PINOCCHIO

CELLOS

Words by NED WASHINGTON
Music by LEIGH HARLINE

Moderately

WHISTLE WHILE YOU WORK

from SNOW WHITE AND THE SEVEN DWARFS

CELLOS

Words by LARRY MOREY
Music by FRANK CHURCHILL